Dedicated to the generations of pupils who inspired these stories by being kind enough to humour me while they were in my classes.

Cover images generated by Copilot

Contents

Chapter 1 - The Classroom

Bloggins ran happily towards his classroom. Other children's classrooms were just ordinary rooms, but Bloggins' classroom was special. As well as his classmates and his beloved teacher, Dr Maggins, it contained all kinds of unusual characters.

There was Bernie the Bin, for example, who loved to be given litter. There was Rodders the Recycling Box, who wanted to be given any rubbish that was made of paper but got very upset if you gave him old rubbers or other stuff that couldn't be recycled easily. In addition, he was keen that the paper you gave him should be flat and not screwed up.

A rival to Rodders, who also wanted to be given paper was Drew the Drawer. Drew's full name was "Drew the Drawer for Perfect Paper", from which you can see that he didn't want just any old paper, but sheets that could be used again by the children for drawing, for instance, or writing the first draft of a poem. It was often a problem for the children to decide whether a piece of paper was more suitable for Drew or for Rodders, as they didn't want to cause unhappiness or jealousy. It was particularly unpleasant if Rodders felt unhappy because then he might sick up pieces of paper all over the floor.

Bernie the Bin was even more prone to be sick, especially if the children's breaktime snacks generated a lot of litter. When Bernie began to feel sick, it was important to try to avoid an accident by giving him Calpol. The kind of Calpol that helped Bernie was a different kind from the liquid that parents tend to give their children. It consisted of someone putting their foot into Bernie and stamping down hard. This usually prevented an unpleasant incident from occurring.

There were other characters in the classroom too, such as Frank the Filing Cabinet, Fergal the Fire Extinguisher, Winston the Wedge and Furry Bag, but I don't want to confuse you by giving you too much information at once and we shall find out more about these and other characters later in the book.

When Bloggins entered the classroom that morning, he was pleased to see that his friends Bliggins and Blaggins were already there. As with most friends, they quite often argued or even fought with each other, but this morning they greeted each other with high fives and shouted "yo"s.

"Shh," said their beloved teacher Dr Maggins. "Gordon the Guitar is with us this morning and he hates to hear a lot of noise. Sit down quietly."

Bloggins, Bliggins and Blaggins sat down, feeling a bit ashamed. They loved it when Gordon the Guitar came to school. They knew he was old, as Dr Maggins had had him since she was a little girl, which was a long time ago, and they also knew that old people don't like to hear a lot of shouting.

Bloggins thought that he might try to apologise to Gordon by bringing him some chocolate the next day. Gordon loved chocolate and was always pleased when children gave him some. Bloggins quite often managed to get his mum to buy him some chocolate to take to Gordon. He had explained to her that Gordon was someone who often visited their class and that he had no arms and no legs. He wondered why his mum's eyes always filled with tears when he told her this, but she was certainly very generous with the chocolate.

After Dr Maggins had taken the register, it was time for Chummy Chat. This happened every morning and the children could talk about "anything in the world" during this time. Lots of hands went up with contributions.

Bloggins' hand went up first. He wanted to tell the class that it was his dad's birthday and that he had made him a sculpture out of twenty-two empty toilet rolls. The other children looked rather concerned about how Bloggins had managed to come by so many toilet rolls and he wasn't sure why Dr Maggins asked him whether everyone in his family was quite well.

Bliggins' turn came next. He told everyone that his mum had bought him yet another nerf gun. Everyone groaned, as this seemed to be Bliggins' obsession and they wondered just how many nerf guns a boy actually needed. Secretly, Dr Maggins knew that Bliggins only had a couple of nerf guns but liked to say he had a new one so he could talk about them in Chummy Chat.

The class groaned again when Blaggins put up his hand. They knew what was coming. Nearly every day Blaggins would either say that he had been to Scunthorpe for the weekend, or that he was planning to go to Scunthorpe the next weekend, or that he was leaving for Scunthorpe that afternoon.

Sometimes Chummy Chat could be quite repetitive, but the children's beloved teacher Dr Maggins always put her head on one side as if concentrating very hard on the information being given, and always managed to say something like "How interesting", even if it was a variation of something they had all heard lots of times before. It was a rule of Chummy Chat that you had to listen politely to everything that was said, without interrupting.

Gordon the Guitar went up to assembly with the children that morning, because he was going to help them to sing a song called "If I were a butterfly". This was one of the children's favourites because it had actions. Gordon couldn't do the actions while he was playing of course, so the children had to do them extra well. They particularly liked the line about the fuzzy wuzzy bear, because the action for that one was to mess your hair up with your fingers.

Dr Maggins loved telling Bible stories. The children regularly had a lesson where she would tell them one. That day, the story was about some people called Adam and Eve, who lived in a garden which Dr Maggins said was the most beautiful garden you would ever have seen. She asked the children if anyone could describe what they thought it would have looked like.

"Totally Minecraft-themed," called out Blaggins.

"What an interesting idea," said Dr Maggins and carried on with the story. Apparently God had told Adam and Eve that they could do whatever they liked in the garden, which was called the Garden of Eden. They could play with the animals or swim in the lake or pick the flowers. But the one thing that they were not allowed to do was to eat the fruit from the tree in the middle of the garden.

One day, when Eve was walking by the tree, she saw a snake curled up in it. The snake was very crafty. He could also talk. The snake pointed out how delicious the forbidden fruit looked and persuaded Eve that nothing bad would happen if she ate some. Eve reached out her hand, picked some of the fruit and took a big bite. She then gave some to Adam, who ate it too. Suddenly, Adam and Eve knew that everything was spoiled. The atmosphere in the garden was no longer happy and peaceful. And they realised something that had been the case all along but hadn't bothered them before - they were stark naked.

The children drew in their breath sharply when they heard this. They could imagine how embarrassing that would be, and they looked down nervously to make sure that they themselves had put some clothes on that morning.

Adam and Eve dived behind a bush. Dr Maggins explained that this was partly so that God wouldn't see them naked but also because their consciences were troubling them about what they had done. Bloggins knew just how this felt. He had hidden in the shed after he had spilled coke on the computer keyboard at home. Bloggins felt particularly guilty because he had been told that he could not have any coke that evening as it would keep him awake. When his mum called him into the living room, he told her that it was not him who had spilled it but his sister, Blogginsina.

"When God called Adam and Eve out from behind the bush and asked if they had eaten the forbidden fruit," went on Dr Maggins, "Adam blamed Eve and Eve blamed the snake."

"How extraordinary," thought Bloggins. "It's as though Dr Maggins read my mind." Apparently he had even more in common with Adam and Eve, Bloggins then discovered, as God was not impressed with their protestations of innocence any more than his mum had been impressed by his. True, the punishment Adam and Eve received from God of being expelled from the Garden of Eden was not quite the same as the one Bloggins had received from his mum, but he resolved to try to be more obedient in the future, as punishments, whatever they were, were no fun.

When Dr Maggins had finished telling the story, she asked the children to write about a time when they had felt tempted and then to draw a picture of the beautiful Garden of Eden. As she felt it might not be a good idea to encourage the children to draw naked people, she suggested that Adam and Eve could be behind the bush.

Bloggins had no difficulty in thinking of what to write, but he couldn't colour his picture because he didn't have any crayons, and he knew his beloved teacher Dr Maggins hated felt tips because she said they made a splodgy mess.

"Can I borrow Furry Bag?" called out Bliggins, and Bloggins realised that this was the solution to his problem too.

Furry Bag was a very kind bag who lived in Dr Maggins' desk drawer. In his tummy were several packets of crayons, which he was generous enough to lend to children who didn't have any of their own. It was important to make sure, though, that you put all the crayons back in Furry Bag's tummy when you had finished with them, and also that they were put in their packets first. If random crayons were put into Furry Bag, they stuck into his tummy and hurt it, and, if any packets were not returned at the end of the lesson, Furry Bag looked and felt very thin. The children loved Furry Bag, and in fact Blaggins had once gone so far as to call out, "Furry Bag kicks ass" when he came out of the drawer. Furry Bag took that as a compliment.

One by one, the children showed their pictures to Dr Maggins. As she looked at each one, Dr Maggins put her head on one side and said, "How lovely," or "What a lovely picture," or "I do like that".

When she came to Bloggins, however, she looked puzzled and pointed to what looked like a yellow and black blob at one side of the picture. Having asked Bloggins what this was, she exclaimed in a slightly forced manner, "Oh a wasp! Well, I suppose there were wasps in the Garden of Eden. It's a lovely wasp."

The lesson ended and it was playtime. The children who had borrowed crayons from Furry Bag carefully put them back in their packets and placed them in Furry Bag's tummy, saying "Thank you, Furry Bag," or giving him a pat. Furry Bag liked good manners and was more likely to lend you his crayons next time if he felt you were grateful for his kindness.

Perhaps you might like to draw a picture here of Bernie the Bin being given Calpol.

Chapter 2 - Furry Bag draws a Rainbow

After playtime a few days later, Bloggins was one of the first to be back in the classroom. He was excited as he knew there would be another Bible story today. But when his beloved teacher Dr Maggins entered, she looked towards Bernie the Bin in horror. Bernie was absolutely full of crisp packets, banana skins, apple cores and sweet wrappers. He was clearly feeling very sick.

"Calpol! Calpol!" yelled Dr Maggins. Bloggins didn't hesitate. He rushed up to Bernie, put his foot inside his tummy and stamped down. Immediately the class breathed a sigh of relief, as all the rubbish that Bernie had been about to vomit onto the floor sank down into his tummy. A nasty moment had been averted, thanks to Bloggins' quick response.

Everyone settled down to listen to today's story. It was about a man called Noah, who was told by God to build an ark. Apparently God was very annoyed with all the people He had made because they were doing lots of bad things. So He had decided to flood the world, wipe them all out and start again. But He had decided to save Noah and his family because they were trying harder to be good.

When Noah had finished the ark, God told him to find a male and a female of every kind of animal and persuade them to get onto the ark. Bloggins gasped. He often had the job of cleaning out the cage of Hammikins 2, the class hamster. (The reason the hamster was called Hammikins 2 was that something quite unpleasant had happened to the first Hammikins, which we won't dwell on here.) While he was doing this, Hammikins 2 was allowed to run about on the floor. It usually proved to be terribly difficult to persuade Hammikins 2 to get back in the cage, so Bloggins wondered how on earth God expected Noah to manage it with all those animals.

To everyone's surprise, all the animals did get on the ark. Dr Maggins explained that God would have helped Noah to persuade them. Bloggins decided he must remember to ask God for help with Hammikins 2 and indeed with other difficult problems. The door of the ark was shut and it started to rain. It rained and it rained. In fact it rained for forty days and forty nights. Bloggins was not surprised by this. He had realised that when you were asked how long something happened for in the Bible, the answer was almost always forty somethings.

When the rain stopped, Noah sent out first a raven and then a dove to see if there was any dry land. The dove came back with an olive twig in its beak. Bloggins knew this was a symbol of peace, as he had been told to offer an olive branch to Bliggins in the playground last week. They had had an argument because Bliggins had called him a fat baboon. Noah opened the door of the ark and everyone got off.

Imagine what it must have been like on the ark with all those animals doing what animals always do a lot of! It would have been much more smelly than Hammikins 2's cage. Noah and his family were so grateful to God for saving them and for letting them be in the fresh air again that they did something that people used to do a lot in those days when they wanted to thank God.

"What do you think it was that they did?" asked Dr Maggins. No one replied. "I'll give you a clue - it began with an s…"

"Sent Him flowers?" suggested Bliggins, remembering what his mum often did after a party.

"Close," said Dr Maggins. "They made a sacrifice. In those days people thought God was up in the sky. We don't think that anymore because most of us have been up in the sky and we don't see God floating by. When they wanted to give God a present, they needed to find something that went up, and the only thing they could think of was smoke. So they would burn something, and I'm afraid it was usually an animal that they had killed. They thought that, as the smoke went up, God was getting their present. That was called making a sacrifice. Anyway, God was really pleased when Noah made his sacrifice and He promised that He would never flood the world again."

"Why on earth would God be pleased to get a burning dead animal?" asked Blaggins in disgust.

"Well, when someone gives you a present, it's the thought that counts," replied Dr Maggins. "I hope that you always remember that when someone gives you a present you don't especially like."

Bloggins felt ashamed that he had not remembered that when Granny gave him a jumper she had knitted for his birthday. It had a picture of a tractor across the front. Perhaps he shouldn't have said that it might be useful for the village scarecrow competition.

"Anyway, God put a sign in the sky so that everyone would always be reminded of His promise when they saw it. It was a rainbow. Rainbows are very beautiful and it's special when you see one because it doesn't happen very often. We'll draw one in a minute, " said Dr Maggins. "The way to remember the colours of the rainbow is to say to yourself, 'Richard of York gave battle in vain'," she went on. "The initial letters of each of those words is the initial letter of one of the colours: red, orange, yellow, green, blue, indigo, violet."

Bloggins looked puzzled. "Where is Vain?" he asked. Dr Maggins hadn't heard his question as she was giving out worksheets about the story and making sure everyone knew they had to do the work in their books. Bloggins thought to himself that perhaps Vain was near Hastings, as he knew there had been a battle there once.

The worksheet contained some questions about the story, a word search, and finally an instruction to draw a rainbow. Luckily Furry Bag contained the necessary colours to do the picture properly and was pleased to have some fresh air when he was lifted out of the drawer of the teacher's desk to help. Each child had a pair of scissors to cut out the word search.

"Give the Shreddies to Rodders," instructed Dr Maggins. Everyone knew that this meant Rodders the Recycling Box would really enjoy the trimmings from the cutting out, so they should not leave them all over the floor.

At the end of the lesson, there were a lot of pieces of the worksheet lying on the tables. Some of the children had doodled on both sides of the paper and others had crumpled or torn it, so they knew that Drew the Drawer would get indigestion if they gave their paper to him. Rodders was very grateful for these Shreddies though. There were several spare worksheets, however, which were still clean and flat, so Drew got a really good meal and looked forward to being useful the next time anyone wanted to draw a picture, perhaps in a wet playtime.

Chapter 3 - Drew the Drawer is Upset

In fact, it looked like rain when the children went out to play the next day. The sky was grey and got darker and darker. Soon big raindrops began to fall. As he ran quickly indoors, Bloggins hoped it was not going to rain for forty days. The classroom was not much like Noah's Ark. Not only did it only have one animal in it (Hammikins 2), but it didn't look as if it would float very well.

The teacher on duty told the children to find something quiet to do in the classroom. Several children wanted to draw, and Drew the Drawer was only too pleased to let the children have pieces of his paper. By good luck, Furry Bag was not asleep in the desk as he usually was, but was out on a table. So he was able to help with the pictures.

Bloggins drew a picture of Bliggins. Unfortunately, because he was not very good at drawing, the boy in the picture was bald, had big ears and was cross-eyed. Bliggins was very upset. He took another piece of paper out of Drew the Drawer and made a paper aeroplane to throw at Bloggins. Bloggins made one too and threw it at Bliggins. Soon there were paper aeroplanes all over the classroom.

Playtime ended and their beloved teacher Dr Maggins came in. When she saw the paper aeroplanes, she was very annoyed. She told Bloggins and Bliggins that it was a shameful waste of paper to use it in that way. She pointed out how upset Drew the Drawer would be. He had been looking after the paper so carefully, keeping it flat and perfect to draw on. It must be terrible for him to see it all creased and wasted. Dr Maggins made Bloggins and Bliggins give the paper aeroplanes to Rodders the Recycling Box. Rodders had not been emptied for a few days, so having all this extra paper, none of which was flat, make him feel sick. Blaggins offered to give him some Calpol.

"After lunch, you must go to the library and write a letter of apology to Drew the Drawer," said Dr Maggins sternly.

Bloggins and Bliggins felt genuinely sorry to have upset Drew so badly. They didn't feel like eating much at lunch and afterwards they went to the library to write their letter. They showed it to Dr Maggins in the classroom later. It said,

"Dear Drew the Drawer, We are very sorry to have wasted your paper by making aeroplanes. We know how important that paper was to you. We can see that now you are quite empty, which must be uncomfortable for you. We will try to save more paper to give you soon and promise not to waste any more. Please forgive us. Sorry again. Love from Bloggins and Bliggins."

Dr Maggins looked as if she was trying not to smile as she read the letter. She put on a stern expression as she returned it to Bloggins and Bliggins and told them to give it to Drew. Luckily the letter had not been folded and so it was just the sort of piece of paper Drew liked. He was obviously very pleased as Bloggins put it into his tummy, in which there was of course a lot of space now.

Bloggins wanted to do more to make amends for his thoughtlessness, so he looked in his tray and was glad to find several old worksheets which were still nice and flat and blank on the back. He gave these to Drew the Drawer and it made him feel less guilty now that he had helped Drew to fill up again.

The children settled down to hear the next Bible story. It was about some brothers called Jacob and Esau. They were twins but not identical ones. Jacob had smooth skin but Esau was very hairy.

"Some men are more hairy than others," explained Dr Maggins. "Has anybody's dad got a hairy chest?"

"My dad has a lot of black hair all round his willy," said Bloggins.

"How interesting," responded Dr Maggins, and moved on quickly with further description of Esau. Apparently he was rough and tough, while Jacob was gentle. Esau liked doing rough and tough things like hunting, but Jacob preferred to help his mum in the kitchen.

One day, the twins' father, Isaac, decided to give Esau a special blessing. Isaac was old and thought he might die soon. Like many old people, he couldn't see or hear very well, and in those days there were no glasses or hearing aids. The blessing was to make sure Esau, who was the older of the twins, became head of the family when Isaac died.

Isaac told Esau to go out and hunt a deer, so that they could eat some venison stew before Isaac gave him the blessing. Because Esau was rough and tough, he went out to do so enthusiastically. Meanwhile Rebecca, the twins' mother, told Jacob she would make some goat stew and he could pretend to be Esau and get the blessing.

"But my father will know I'm not Esau because I look different," protested Jacob.

"That doesn't matter because your father is…"

"Blind!" shouted Bliggins.

"And I sound different," went on Jacob.

"That doesn't matter because your father is…"

"Deaf!" shouted Blaggins.

"But suppose my father touches me?" asked Jacob.

Rebecca tied some goat skin onto Jacob's arms so that he would feel hairy. Jacob took the stew into Isaac's room and tried to put on a rough and tough, deep voice when he said,

"Here I am, Father. I've brought the stew made from a deer I caught. Let's eat it, then you can give me your blessing."

Isaac ate the stew. Apparently he couldn't tell the difference between venison stew and goat stew, but he was a bit confused about which of his sons had brought it to him.

"I can't see you," he said, "so come closer and let me touch you." Jacob nervously came closer and his father touched his arms. Apparently Isaac could not tell the difference between touching goat skin and touching a rough and tough person's hairy arm either, so he gave Jacob the blessing.

When Esau came home and found out what had happened, he was absolutely…

"Furious!" yelled Bloggins. Esau said he was going to kill Jacob. But Rebecca had already thought that might happen, so, before Esau came home, she had packed Jacob's bag and told him to go and stay with his Uncle Laban, who lived across the desert.

The children were keen to write down what they thought of the way everyone had behaved in the story. When they had finished their writing, they brought it to their beloved teacher Dr Maggins, who took Peter Pan the Pen out of Horace the Handbag to draw lots of red ticks and write "Good" at the bottom of each piece.

She then gave each pupil a picture of Isaac and Jacob and told them to stick a piece of cotton wool on Jacob's arms. This seemed to Bloggins to be an odd thing to do. Could Isaac really not tell the difference between a rough and tough man's hairy arms and a piece of cotton wool? He did his best with his picture, but of course he was not very good at drawing so it wasn't really clear where Jacob's arms actually were. He stuck his piece of cotton wool rather randomly onto Jacob.

When Bliggins looked at Bloggins' picture, he started to snigger. He called Blaggins over to look at where Bloggins had stuck his piece of cotton wool. Alerted by their laughter, Dr Maggins asked to see the picture. When she saw it, Bloggins was pleased to see the corners of her mouth turn upwards. She obviously liked it a lot.

"What a lovely picture," Dr Maggins said enthusiastically to Bloggins. "But, as visitors might look at your book, I think it will look even better if we remove the cotton wool and give it to Bernie."

What do you think Bloggins' picture of Bliggins looked like?

Chapter 4 - Winston the Wedge is Needed

Bloggins was excited during registration a few days later, as he had something very interesting to contribute to Chummy Chat. His hand shot up as soon as he heard that Chummy Chat was starting.

"My sister Blogginsina has told me that it is Hammikins 2's birthday next week. Can we give him a party?"

"Ooh yes," called out Bliggins, forgetting you have to put up your hand if you want to say something in Chummy Chat. "I could bring Fang, my hamster, and Blaggins could bring his hamster, Dougal, and we could let them play party games like the ones we played at Christmas."

Their beloved teacher Dr Maggins looked doubtful, and asked if anyone else had something they'd like to contribute to Chummy Chat, reminding them that they could talk about "anything in the world".

Bliggins wanted to tell the class that he had dropped one of his nerf guns out of the window last night.

"How interesting," said Dr Maggins.

Blaggins wanted to say that his family were going to Scunthorpe at the weekend. Everyone groaned and even Dr Maggins had difficulty looking interested.

Bloggins put up his hand again.

"There's a very funny smell over here," he said, wrinkling his nose. Everyone looked at Bliggins. Bliggins went red and tried to look as if the smell was coming from Blaggins.

"We must open the door and let some fresh air in," said Dr Maggins, who always knew the best way to deal with any problem. "Where is Winston the Wedge?"

Winston the Wedge was a triangular piece of wood who lived near the door. In the winter, he had rather a boring life, because the door was usually kept closed to keep in the warmth. Because he wasn't needed much, he often found himself being kicked under the coats or behind a cupboard, which made him feel depressed and unloved. However, in the summer, his life improved enormously, as he was frequently asked to hold open the classroom door in order to try and keep the room cool.

Winston got very excited when he heard that he was needed to deal with an unpleasant smell. Unfortunately, it took the children a little while to find him, as he was squashed between Frank the Filing Cabinet and the cupboard known as Rose Cottage.

"Here he is!" exclaimed Bloggins, picking Winston up and waving him triumphantly. He opened the door and wedged Winston underneath it. Winston felt important. Gradually fresh air began to replace the smell.

Feeling a little bit chilly, the children settled down to listen to today's story. They were eager to find out what happened to Jacob after he left home. They remembered that his mother, Rebecca, had told him to walk across the desert to the place where his uncle Laban lived.

A desert is called a desert because it tends to be deserted. Jacob trudged across this one feeling lonelier and lonelier and more and more guilty. He did a lot of thinking as there was no one to talk to, and he felt very very sorry that he had been so unkind by playing a trick on his old, blind father.

One night, Jacob lay down to sleep with his head on a stone, which he had chosen to use as a pillow.

"Ugh," interrupted Bloggins. "That must have been really uncomfortable. I'd have used my bag or a pile of sand."

"Yes, or a duvet," called out Bliggins. Everyone groaned, as they knew Jacob hadn't brought a duvet with him. Bliggins felt embarrassed again.

Perhaps it was because he was uncomfortable that Jacob had a strange dream. In the dream, he saw a ladder stretching up to heaven. Angels were climbing up and down the ladder, and Jacob heard God telling him that he was forgiven for his unkind trick. When he woke up, Jacob felt a lot better and he continued on his way to Uncle Laban's house, which wasn't far away now.

Everyone was keen to hear what happened when Jacob arrived at Uncle Laban's house. It must have been a surprise for Uncle Laban, as of course Jacob had not been able to text or email to say he was coming.

Before continuing, however, Dr Maggins asked the children to write a few sentences about Jacob's dream. It did not take long for most of them to do so and they were soon queuing up at Dr Maggins' desk for her to mark what they had written. It was time for

Peter Pan the Pen to wake up. He was asleep in Horace the Handbag, but now he got up, ready to mark the children's work. He had recently been ill with a complaint that meant no ink came out of him. During that time, another pen called Ruby Red had taken his place. Peter Pan the Pen thought Ruby Red's ink was much too bright, and he was pleased when a refill was put into his tummy and he felt better and able to take over the marking again.

Dr Maggins was a super-fast reader. She scanned each piece of writing and asked Peter Pan the Pen to write "Good" at the bottom of them all; until she came to Bloggins.

Bloggins had written, "Jacob was asleep in the dessert. He saw angles on a ladder."

His beloved teacher Dr Maggins started to smile. "Asleep in the dessert?" she queried. "Wouldn't that be a trifle messy?" The children laughed. "I'm glad there were angles on the ladder though," Dr Maggins went on, "otherwise it might have collapsed into the dessert and that really would have made an awful mess."

Peter Pan the Pen wrote, "You have tried to finish too quickly. Take more care next time." Bloggins knew Peter Pan the Pen did not like having to write this sort of thing. His favourite things to write were "Excellent" or "Good". Peter Pan the Pen now felt tired after writing so much and went back to sleep in Horace the Handbag while the children found out what happened at Uncle Laban's house.

Uncle Laban was delighted to welcome Jacob, whom he hadn't seen since Jacob was a little boy. Now Jacob was a man, and he found that his cousins had grown up too. Laban's younger daughter, Rachel, was beautiful and sweet-natured. Jacob wanted to marry her. Uncle Laban said that he could do so, but must work for him for seven years first. Jacob wanted to marry Rachel so badly that he agreed.

At the end of the seven years, there was a wedding. But, when the bride drew back her veil, to his horror Jacob realised that it was not Rachel but her older sister, Leah. Uncle Laban had tricked him into marrying the wrong girl.

"Oh that's not fair!" complained Jacob, forgetting that it was not long ago that he himself had played a trick.

Uncle Laban was sorry, but he had wanted his older daughter to be married before his younger one. He had thought someone would have wanted to marry Leah during the seven years, but no one had, so he played the trick.

"But don't worry," he said to Jacob. "You can marry Rachel as well."

In those days, men were allowed to have as many wives as they wanted. They didn't have to get divorced before they married someone else like people have to do now. Sadly it didn't work that way for girls though; they could only have one husband each.

"Yay!" shouted Blaggins, while the girls in the class looked upset. Life was very sexist in Bible times.

Anyway, Jacob did eventually marry Rachel as well, but first Uncle Laban made him work for another seven years.

"Gosh, I wouldn't work for fourteen years to marry anyone!" said Bloggins. "I'd have got fed up after a few weeks and found another girlfriend."

"Fancy wanting to marry a girl at all," Bliggins chimed in. "Girls are soppy."

An argument broke out.

"The fact that Jacob was prepared to work for fourteen years in order to marry Rachel shows how much he loved her," replied Dr Maggins loudly and firmly. "And that is very important for understanding the next story, which is one I think you will know if you have seen the musical 'Joseph and his amazing technicolour dreamcoat.'"

Everyone started to talk about when they had seen the musical, and Bloggins began to sing "Give me my coloured coat, my amazing coloured coat", not very tunefully. At the same time, the children started to realise that they felt really rather cold. Winston the Wedge was still holding the door open, and they had been enjoying the lesson so much that they had forgotten about him.

"Shut the door please, Bliggins," said Dr Maggins.

Bliggins gave Winston the Wedge a kick. Winston fell over and the door swung shut. Winston felt sad that no one ever gave him any chocolate, paper or Calpol, only kicks. But, as he snuggled under the children's coats, he felt it had been a good day because he had been able to be useful.

Chapter 5 - Hammikins 2 has a Party

Tuesday of next week was going to be an exciting day, as it was Hammikins 2's birthday. Blogginsina had told Bloggins that last year they had had a party for Hammikins 2 instead of History. Gordon the Guitar had come to school and had helped the children to sing several of Hammikins 2's favourite songs. These included "Old Macdonald had a farm, e-i-e-i-o, and on that farm he had a hamster, e-i-e-i-o", and "Daddy's taking us to the zoo tomorrow - See all the hamsters scritch-scritch-scratching", and a hymn which had a verse beginning, "When God made the hamster of creation, He filled it full of His love". Blogginsina had brought in a chocolate cake and everyone had had a great time.

Bloggins was determined that this year Hammikins 2 would have an even better birthday party. He had asked his mum to make a special cake of bits of carrot and lettuce held together in jelly, and that morning he took this into school, together with his own hamster, Brutus.

When he arrived, he was pleased to see that Bliggins had brought Fang and Blaggins had brought Dougal. Before registration, they introduced all the hamsters to each other through the bars of the cages.

When their beloved teacher Dr Maggins arrived, the boys were surprised to see that she didn't look all that pleased to see so many hamsters. Gordon the Guitar was with her, and she seemed to think that Hammikins 2's party would be similar to the one he had last year.

"But it will be much nicer for Hammikins 2 to have some hamster guests at his party," said Bloggins during Chummy Chat. "And I think he will like this cake much more than the chocolate cake he was given last year, which my sister told me made his fur all sticky."

Dr Maggins looked doubtful, but said Brutus, Fang and Dougal were very welcome so long as the children concentrated on their lessons and didn't get them out of their cages at any time. Gordon the Guitar was looking forward to the party, which would take place during the last lesson, just before the children went home.

The Bible story that day was about someone called Moses. He was trying to lead some people called the Israelites through a desert between Egypt and a country that was then called the Promised Land because the people were sure God had promised it to them.

"How long do you think the Israelites were in the desert?" asked Dr Maggins.

Bloggins remembered which number was always the answer to this sort of question.

"Forty days?" he suggested.

Dr Maggins was pleased that Bloggins had remembered the number forty, but said that in this case the answer was forty years. She went on to say that, some years ago, she had herself been on holiday in the very same desert, which, although deserted in Bible times, now has places such as Sharm-el-Sheikh in it. When it was time to go home, all the flights were cancelled because of a volcano that had erupted in Iceland. No one knew when it would be safe for aeroplanes to be in the air again and Dr Maggins was afraid she might have to stay in the desert for forty years like the Israelites, but luckily the flights started again a week later.

During that week, all the people behaved well but, when the Israelites were there in Bible times, they behaved very badly. Moses tried to keep them in order but he didn't have a list of rules that he could tell them they had to obey.

So God told Moses to climb up a mountain, which was actually more like a hill, called Mount Sinai. He was at the top for, you've guessed it, forty days, and, while he was there, God gave him two tablets of stone with ten rules carved into them. The rules were called the Ten Commandments and people still think they are important today. Four of them are about how to treat God and the other six are about how to treat other people. Even people who don't believe in God think the last six are important. They say that you must respect your parents, that you should be content with what you have, that you mustn't lie, steal or murder, or break up families by being unfaithful to your husband or wife.

Dr Maggins asked the children to write down some suggestions of other commandments that they thought were important to keep today. Drew the Drawer kindly let everyone have a piece of his paper so they could do this.

Afterwards, Dr Maggins read out some of their ideas. There were lots of good ones about turning lights off when you left the room, picking up litter, trying to use less plastic, and walking or cycling to places instead of getting your parents to drive short distances. Rodders was delighted that many of the other ideas were about recycling, which of course was terribly important to him.

Peter Pan the Pen gave lots of ticks and wrote "Good ideas" a number of times. When he came to Bloggins' ideas, however, he was not sure what to put, so he just wrote "How interesting." Bloggins' list said:

"Do not pick your nose.
Do not be sick on people.
Do not look at other people's privets."

When Moses came down from Mount Sinai, he gathered all the Israelites together and read them the Ten Commandments. They made a covenant with God that they would try to keep these rules.

"Who remembers what a covenant is?" asked Dr Maggins.

Bliggins' hand shot up. He remembered hearing about this in another lesson.

"It's a place where nuns live!" he replied.

Everyone sniggered. Dr Maggins explained that what Bliggins was thinking of was a convent. A covenant is in fact an agreement or a deal. The Israelites were making a deal with God that He would look after them if they tried to behave themselves.

Now that the story was over, it was time for Hammikins 2's birthday party. The children made a circle of chairs and placed the four hamster cages on some desks in the middle. Gordon the Guitar took his coat off and got his music ready. Everyone was very excited.

First of all, Bloggins got out the carrrot-in-jelly cake that he had brought in. His mum hadn't had a mould in the shape of a hamster, so the cake was rabbit-shaped, but Hammikins 2, Brutus, Fang and Dougal didn't seem to mind. Bloggins put spoonfuls into their cages and, while they didn't seem especially keen on the jelly, they enjoyed finding the bits of carrot and lettuce. None of the children fancied Bloggins' cake much, but luckily someone had brought some chocolate biscuits. These were really for Gordon, but there were enough for everyone and Gordon was happy to share them.

The party was really going with a swing and Bloggins felt that it was time for some party games. Dr Maggins looked rather worried as the children took the hamsters out of their cages so that they could join in. First they played musical statues. The hamsters didn't seem entirely to get the hang of this game and were all out quite quickly, but each of them sat on someone's lap until the game was over.

"What shall we play next?" asked Bloggins.

"Let's play 'The farmer's in his den'," suggested Bliggins, who had recently enjoyed playing this at a party.

"Good idea!" shouted Bloggins and, before Gordon could find the right music, the children were singing the song and adding the hamsters to the middle one by one. Because it was his birthday, Hammikins 2 was the farmer. Bloggins thought Brutus looked a bit dismayed to be chosen as the farmer's wife in the second verse. For the third verse, Fang was chosen as the child and Dougal was added to the group for the dog in the next verse. The children's singing became louder and more raucous for each verse as they were enjoying the game so much. So they didn't hear their beloved teacher Dr Maggins calling out that they should stop the game at once.

You probably know that books and websites about keeping hamsters say things like, "You must keep a Syrian hamster by itself. Putting two Syrian hamsters together means war." Dr Maggins remembered this and very soon the children did too. As Bloggins placed the farmer, his wife and child on Dougal for the verse "We all pat the dog", all the hamsters bared their teeth and a terrible fight broke out.

The excited singing changed to squeals of terror as the party boy started to bite his guests. Some of the children began to cry. Without thinking, Bloggins pulled the hamsters apart and threw some books between them. His courageous action stopped Hammikins 2 from inflicting any serious injury on the other hamsters, but poor Bloggins got a nasty bite on his finger.

As Bloggins was bleeding and obviously in pain, his kindly teacher Dr Maggins did not like to sound as cross as she felt, but she ordered that all the hamsters should be put back in their cages at once and sent Bloggins to the nurse to have his wound disinfected and bandaged. A couple of the hamsters had some blood on them and Dr Maggins advised that their owners should take them to the vet after school.

The party was spoilt. What a pity. Gordon the Guitar was very upset that he hadn't had a chance to play Hammikins 2's favourite songs and his music was put firmly back into Frank the Filing Cabinet. Dr Maggins made a covenant with the children that Gordon would only get his music out again another day if they promised to think and listen a lot more carefully in future.

Hammikins 2 would love you to draw a picture of him on this page.

Chapter 6 - Fergal the Fire Extinguisher's Sad History

The weeks passed. The weather became warmer, which made Winston the Wedge very happy as he was often needed to hold the door open. He was hardly ever kicked under the coats or forced to sit between Frank the Filing Cabinet and Rose Cottage for days on end. He tried to make sure he was always ready beside the door. However, he did sometimes hide under the coats, because he enjoyed hearing someone call out,

"Where's Winston the Wedge?"

It made him feel important.

Someone else who always hoped he might be needed for the important job of holding the door open was Fergal the Fire Extinguisher. A few years ago, the children used to move him from the corner to prop the door open when the weather was hot.

However, Fergal the Fire Extinguisher was not only rather heavy and difficult to move, he also had a black hose coming out of his shoulder and reaching down to where it fitted into a slot at his bottom. When the children heaved him in front of the door, the hose quite often came out of the slot and waved about.

Disaster struck one day when Dr Maggins had spent a long time putting up a display of work that the children had done. It was a special display of particularly careful work that the children had done by hand, ready for a time a few days later when a great many visitors were likely to be coming round the school.

The weather was hot that week. When the children came in from playtime, they were sweating and red in the face from running about. No teacher had arrived yet, so they decided, unsupervised, to prop the door open with Fergal the Fire Extinguisher. Fergal was standing across the room from the door, with the Special Display on the wall in between.

"I'll carry Fergal the Fire Extinguisher over to the door," called out someone. She grabbed Fergal by his hose and started to pull. Of course the hose came out of its slot, and when Fergal had been dragged halfway across the room, he began to feel quite unwell and just couldn't manage to stand upright anymore.

To the children's horror, not only did Fergal fall over, but the entire contents of his stomach squirted out of the hose and all over the Special Display. One girl tried to pull Fergal further away from the wall, but this only resulted in the hose spraying a wider area of it. Everyone stood transfixed, staring at the terrible damage that was being done to the work. It had been written in fountain pen and illustrated with felt tips. All the ink started to run together and drip down in blotches and streaks. The Special Display was ruined.

It would be better not to describe in too much detail the reaction of their beloved but already harassed teacher Dr Maggins when she entered the room and saw what had happened. It is probably enough to say that all the children were put into detention for several days running until they had redone the work. Fergal the Fire Extinguisher, too, was in disgrace. He felt this was most unfair as he had not fallen over and been sick on purpose. Although he was always happy to help by propping the door open, he had not asked to be pulled across the room. He had tried to say that the children should wait for a teacher, but no one had listened.

Nevertheless, Fergal was punished by being fixed permanently to a wall so that he could no longer be used to prop the door open. His tummy was refilled and every so often, a man would come round and check that his hose and nozzle were in the right place, as Fergal was not trusted now to look after himself. He felt very upset.

It was not long after this happened that Winston the Wedge came to live in the classroom. Fergal's humiliation was complete. He was not even needed now to do what he believed to be his most important job. The children tried to tell him that in fact he had a much more important job, namely to make sure no one got burned if the classroom caught fire, but that, sadly, never seemed to happen.

Anyway, on this particular hot day, when Winston the Wedge had been put in place, the children gathered round for the Bible story. By this time, they had moved on to the second part of the Bible, called the New Testament (not the "Young Testament" as someone had suggested when Dr Maggins had told them they were moving on from the Old Testament and asked what they thought the next part was called). They had heard the story about Jesus being born and were now learning about his cousin, whose name was John the Baptist.

John was called the Baptist because, when he grew up, he spent a lot of time standing by the River Jordan - (can you find out where that is?) - calling out to people that they ought to be sorry about all the bad things they had done. A lot of people listened to him and did feel sorry, so then they waded into the river and John baptised them. That means he helped them go under the water and up again straight away, so that their sins, or bad deeds, would be washed away.

When he heard this, Bloggins looked confused.

"Does that mean there were then lots of sins floating about in the river?" he asked.

"What an interesting question," replied Dr Maggins. "No. The sins weren't literally sticking onto the people when they went into the river, so they weren't floating about in it afterwards. Baptism is a symbolic way of God saying he forgives someone - just like when I give you a star it is a symbolic way of saying I am pleased with you."

John had rather a strange way of life. Because he wanted to concentrate on God all the time, he didn't want to waste time worrying about what to wear or what to eat. So he always wore a tunic made out of a camel skin and he always ate locusts and wild honey.

"Ugh!" said Bliggins.

John was trying to get people ready for the time Jesus turned up. The people were expecting a special saviour called the Messiah to come and help them, and John knew this was Jesus and that Jesus would hope to find people trying to be good. One day, Jesus did turn up at the river. He waded in and John baptised him.

"Didn't Jesus get Weil's Disease?" blurted out Bloggins. The children had been on a Science trip recently where they had been told to wear wellingtons and rubber gloves, as teachers have to think of everything that could possibly go wrong on trips and there was a remote possibility of getting this nasty disease when they were taking specimens of water. The Science teacher had reassured them that this was only a precaution but Bloggins had made sure he wore two pairs of rubber gloves, a yellow one inside a pink one, just in case.

Dr Maggins assured him that Jesus did not get Weil's Disease. On the contrary, when he came up out of the water, a dove was seen hovering over him and

God's voice was heard saying that Jesus was His beloved Son.

When the story was finished, the children were asked to draw a picture of John baptising Jesus. Furry Bag was asked to come out of the drawer in order to help with the colouring. Furry Bag had been having a lovely dream about being magically filled with crayons made of real gold and silver, so he wasn't very happy about being woken up. But, being a kind bag, he had soon lent out all his crayons and the pictures were brought to the teacher's desk for Peter Pan the Pen to mark.

When Dr Maggins examined Bloggins' picture, she had a puzzled look on her face. There was a shape in the river with a wide V above its head that was obviously meant to be Jesus with the dove hovering over him, which was fine, but there was something about John's appearance that looked very strange. In Bloggins' picture, he seemed to have enormous breasts.

"I don't think you will find that John the Baptist had enormous breasts," Dr Maggins told Bloggins. "Why have you drawn him like that?"

"Well," replied Bloggins, "you told us that John the Baptist wore a tunic made out of a camel skin."

"Yes, that's right," said Dr Maggins, "but I still don't understand why you have drawn him like this."

"Those are the camel's humps," explained Bloggins patiently.

Chapter 7 - Bloggins is Hot

That summer seemed to be a particularly hot one. Winston the Wedge was in constant use, but everybody still felt extremely hot, especially after they had been running about. One afternoon, when they had been doing this during playtime, Bloggins had a really good idea. He took a piece of paper out of Drew the Drawer and folded it into a concertina shape to make a fan. He started to waft this backwards and forwards near his face.

Everyone else admired Bloggins' invention, which seemed to have a lot more immediate use than most of the things teachers asked them to make in lessons. Bliggins took a piece of paper out of Drew and copied Bloggins' idea. Blaggins did the same and then everyone started to jostle round Drew, trying to get out the next piece of his paper. Poor Drew was very worried, partly because he didn't want to run out of paper and partly because he didn't want anyone to get hurt.

"My fan is too small," called out Bliggins. "Has Drew got any A3-sized paper?"

"Yes, good idea," shouted Blaggins. "I remember there is some underneath the smaller pieces from when we were given that illustrated timeline in History."

Bliggins and Blaggins tried to push the other children out of the way and both grabbed at the bigger pieces of paper at the bottom of the drawer. Everybody was pushing and shoving and of course it wasn't long before someone fell over and banged her lip on Drew's corner. She started to cry when she saw it was bleeding. Drew felt awful. He certainly hadn't meant to hurt the little girl with his corner.

When their beloved teacher Dr Maggins came in, she found a riot going on. Everyone was shouting or pushing or crying or bleeding. But what really made her cross, as I'm sure you can guess, was the number of pieces of previously perfect paper that had been pulled out of Drew to make fans. They all had to be cleared up and put carefully into Rodders before the story.

Bloggins offered to do this. He felt guilty because he had started the fan idea, even though he had not been doing any of the fighting. Dr Maggins was pleased and thanked him, as of course it is important always to thank someone who does something kind.

Today's Bible story was on that subject - thanking people, not making fans. Jesus was walking through the countryside one day when he passed ten men who had a horrible disease called leprosy. Lepers, as they were called, were not welcome in towns and villages, because people were scared of catching their disease. They had to ring a bell and call out "Unclean!" as they walked along so that ordinary people knew they were coming and could make sure they didn't go anywhere near them.

Jesus felt sorry for the lepers, as they had such miserable lives as well as feeling ill. When Jesus met sick people, he often healed them, and he did this to the ten lepers. He told them to go and show themselves to the priests, who would tell them that they could mix with everyone again now. They were, of course, all absolutely thrilled. They could hardly believe they were better, and they ran off to find their family and friends so that they could tell them what happened.

But one of the lepers hadn't got far when he turned round and came back to Jesus.

"Thank you very much for healing me," he said.

Jesus was very pleased that the leper had come back to thank him, but he was disappointed that the other nine did not. Even when you are excited, it is still important to remember to say thank you.

Bloggins had finished clearing up the paper. He had managed, though, not to put his own fan into Rodders and had begun to waft it backwards and forwards again, as he still felt hot.

"Are you listening to the story, Bloggins?" asked Dr Maggins sharply, as she had noticed his fanning for the first time.

"Yes, yes!" replied Bloggins quickly, trying to hide his fan behind his back.

"So who did Jesus meet coming towards him ringing a bell?" asked Dr Maggins suspiciously.

Bloggins tried to think back to what he had only half heard.
"A leopard," he blurted out.

Everybody laughed. Dr Maggins was cross and said that Bloggins had better stay in during the next break to draw a picture of ten leopards ringing bells.

At St Joggins, there was a system of giving "stars" to pupils who pleased the teachers by doing a particularly good piece of work, or trying especially hard, or being noticeably helpful or well behaved. Those pupils who had not wasted Drew's paper by making fans and had then listened attentively to the story were each given a star at the end of the lesson.

The stars were actually round stickers. If you were given one, you had to peel off the backing and stick the star in your star book. Children often left the small pieces of backing paper lying around the room so, in order to stop them from doing this, Bernie the Bin had made it known that he was particularly fond of coffee and that he was always pleased if he was given some.

Of course, Bernie was getting a bit confused between the words "star backs" and "Starbucks", but the children knew that if they were reminded to give Bernie some coffee, it meant that they were supposed to put their star backs into his tummy instead of making a mess by leaving them on the desks and floor. Those children who had been given stars at the end of this lesson remembered to give Bernie the coffee before they went out to play.

"I hope Bernie won't get too high on all that caffeine," remarked Bloggins rather ruefully. He felt a bit upset that not only had he not been given a star but he had to stay in during break to draw the leopards.

Because Dr Maggins was an exceptionally kind teacher, she realised that Bloggins and the others had only been trying to make fans because they were so uncomfortably hot, and that something needed to be done about this. Winston the Wedge was doing his best to keep the room cool, but it was just too much for him. So it was the next day that Finn the Fan came to live in the classroom.

Chapter 8 - Finn the Fan is Mischievous

Having Finn the Fan joining the characters in the classroom was a bit of a mixed blessing. All the children wanted to sit close to him so that they could feel the breeze that he made cooling their faces. Obviously there wasn't room for everyone to do this and the further away from Finn the Fan you were, the less you could feel him. The children at the back, who tended to be the good children who could be trusted to get on with their work sensibly, couldn't really feel Finn the Fan at all and still felt very hot.

When their beloved teacher Dr Maggins wasn't looking, some children stood very close to Finn the Fan and were even stupid enough to try to push their fingers through his grill. Luckily the bars of his grill were too close together for them to get their fingers right in for, if they had managed to do so, Finn the Fan would have bitten their fingers right off!

Finn the Fan was actually rather a mischievous fan. He loved to try and blow the papers off the desks of the children sitting in the front row. These children tended to be the ones who were only too pleased if something happened to stop them from getting on with their work, so Finn the Fan was often in disgrace for distracting them in this way.

It was another very hot day when the children heard the story of how Jesus chose his first disciples. Winston the Wedge was doing his best to keep the room cool, but a lot of the children still felt uncomfortable as the story began.

Jesus chose twelve disciples altogether. His disciples were his special friends who helped him in his work as the Son of God and carried on with it after he wasn't with them anymore. Jesus only chose men to be his disciples which Dr Maggins explained was one of the reasons some people don't think ladies ought to be vicars and priests. Dr Maggins herself thought an important reason Jesus only chose men was that ladies in those days had to stay at home to look after their families and so wouldn't have been able to travel round with Jesus in the way he wanted his disciples to do.

"The word disciple actually means a pupil," she went on. "It comes from the Latin word for a pupil. So in fact you are all my disciples today."

Dr Maggins' disciples smiled and looked forward to hearing how Jesus had chosen his first ones.

Jesus had been walking by the Sea of Galilee, which is in the north of Israel and, despite its name, is in fact a lake, when he saw some fishermen washing their nets. He got into the boat of one of them, a man named Simon, and suggested he went out fishing with them.

Simon looked unimpressed, "That's a silly idea," he whinged. "We've been fishing all night and haven't caught anything. But I suppose, if you really want to, we could try again," he went on grudgingly.

"Simon sounds just like Eeyore," remarked Bloggins. The Head Teacher of St Joggins was a fan of the Winnie-the-Pooh stories and had recently been talking to the children about how people can choose to be Tiggers or Eeyores in life. Tigger, as you'll no doubt know, was always bouncy and optimistic. Everything to him was potentially exciting and he wanted to try whatever was on offer. Eeyore of course was completely the opposite. He saw the world in a negative way. He expected things to go wrong and wasn't surprised when they did. The Head had asked the children to ask themselves whether they were more like Tigger or Eeyore and which they thought would be the most helpful attitude for going through life.

Bloggins had thought carefully about this. He tried to be a Tigger himself and was always ready to point out Eeyores - hence his comment about Simon.

"Eeyore! Eeyore!" called out Bliggins and Blaggins, taking up the theme.

Dr Maggins ignored them and continued with the story.

Simon sailed the boat out into the centre of the lake. He and his brother cast their net into the water and waited. They did not have to wait long. Soon hundreds of fish had swum into the net. In fact there were so many that Simon and Andrew couldn't fit them all into their boat and had to ask their friends James and John to help. It was absolutely extraordinary.

Simon was quite frightened, as he couldn't think how Jesus had managed to do this. Jesus told him not to be afraid, as he wanted Simon to become one of his disciples and help him to "fish for men". This was not as weird as it sounds. Jesus meant that he wanted Simon to help him to bring people closer to God.

Simon and Andrew, James and John left their boats, their nets and all those fish and followed Jesus. Dr

Maggins advised the class that, if a strange man came up to any of them and asked them to follow him, they definitely shouldn't do so. But there was obviously something very special about Jesus that made people want to be with him. Jesus gave Simon a new name, Peter, because petros is Greek for a rock (think about the words "petrol" and "petrified") and Jesus said he was going to build his church on Simon Peter.

"That sounds really painful!" exclaimed Bloggins. But Jesus didn't mean he was literally going to build a church on Peter. Although we think of a church as being a building, its proper meaning is a group of Christians and it was Peter who eventually shaped the first Christians into an organisation. He became the first Pope and St Peter's Basilica in Rome is named after him.

Dr Maggins had a book of cut-out models of some of the Bible stories. She gave everyone a copy of the one about the fishermen and asked them to cut out and make the model of the boat, which would contain Simon Peter and lots of fish.

The children started to cut out the pieces. Bloggins decided that, instead of cutting round the net, which had a picture of lots of fish inside it, he would cut out all the fish separately. He thought this would look more realistic. He got to work. Soon his desk was covered in lots of little fish, which were printed on thin card.

"I'm really hot," called out Bliggins when they had been working for some time.

"So am I," said Blaggins, "I'm sweating". The sun was shining straight through the window now and everyone was feeling uncomfortable.

Winston the Wedge was trying hard, but Finn the Fan was obviously needed. Without thinking, Bloggins got up and switched Finn the Fan onto his highest setting.

Finn the Fan was delighted. This was going to be fun. Soon the boats and disciples that had been cut out by the children in the front desks had been blown onto the floor. Finn the Fan was enjoying himself. His head started to swivel from side to side, and it wasn't long before his breath reached Bloggins' desk. All Bloggins' fish whirled up into the air.

"Ooh, flying fish!" screeched Bloggins, and his friends ran up to his desk trying to catch them. Everyone was laughing. The fish were getting everywhere - some were in children's hair and some were flying out of the window. The children in the front desks scrabbled on the floor, trying to pick up their bits of boat and disciple.

It was several days before all the fish had been found and picked up. Rodders the Recycling Box and Bernie the Bin enjoyed the small fishy snacks that kept coming their way.

Finn the Fan was in disgrace. He was firmly switched off, unplugged and moved into a corner. He didn't really mind though. He knew that in that hot summer the class would not be able to do without his services for long and he smirked to himself as he wondered what havoc he would be able to create next time.

*Can you draw a picture of Winston the Wedge
holding the door open?*

Chapter 9 - Bernie the Bin is Sunburnt

It wasn't only the children who were affected by the hot sunny weather, as everyone discovered the next time they had Chummy Chat.

The first hands to go up were those of Bliggins and Blaggins as usual. You will be able to guess the subject of what each of them wanted to say. Bliggins wanted to tell everyone that he had put up a target in his garden the previous evening in order to practise shooting with his nerf guns. On the target, he had drawn pictures of Bloggins, Blaggins and a few of the other children in the class.

"I managed to hit all of you," he announced proudly, looking round for some admiration. No one looked very interested, but Bliggins didn't seem to notice. He was about to say more, but Dr Maggins quickly asked Blaggins what he wanted to say, as if she didn't know.

"My mum says that when we go to Scunthorpe at the weekend, we can spend a day at the seaside. I am looking forward to building sandcastles with my new bucket and spade. I am calling them Boff and Spiff," said Blaggins excitedly.

"How interesting," said Dr Maggins rather wearily. "I hope you have a lovely time."

As it was a rule of Chummy Chat that you could talk about "anything in the world" and everyone knew they had to listen politely to every contribution, Bliggins and Blaggins always looked forward to having a captive audience at every session.

Bloggins was now waving his hand in the air, clearly bursting with something he'd noticed.

"Look at Bernie the Bin!" he called out. "He's got sunburnt!"

Everyone looked at Bernie the Bin and gasped in surprise. Usually Bernie was a grey colour, but today he was bright red! He seemed to be a slightly different shape too and everyone looked worried.

"Poor Bernie! He is obviously feeling really uncomfortable and poorly," said Bloggins.

"Silly Bernie," chipped in Bliggins. "He obviously didn't listen to the talk the Nurse gave us about sun safety. He must have gone outside without a hat or sun cream."

"Don't be mean to Bernie," said Blaggins. "He's only a bin and he probably didn't know any better. When my mum thinks we have been in the sun too much, she rubs after-sun lotion on us. You ought to do that to Bernie, Dr Maggins."

Dr Maggins felt that she might get some funny looks if the Head or indeed anyone else came in and found her rubbing after-sun lotion into her bin, so she changed the subject by starting today's story.

Jesus knew that the religious leaders wanted to kill him. He was very popular with most of the ordinary people. They loved the stories that he told to explain what God was really like, and were impressed by the way that he treated people. We are used to the idea that everyone should be treated equally. It wasn't like that when Jesus was alive, but he was kind and welcoming to everyone, especially people like lepers, beggars or women, who were usually treated as inferior. Also, he had an amazing ability to heal people who were blind, or deaf or lame or, on a few occasions, even dead! No wonder hundreds of people flocked to him wherever he went, and no wonder the religious leaders were jealous.

The religious leaders had always taught people that God was very fierce and that you had to be very careful not to annoy Him because if you did He would zap you. Jesus said this was completely wrong. He described God as being like a loving father.

Bloggins liked this idea better. He knew that his father always forgave him if he said he was sorry for something he'd done wrong, and was not rubbing his hands together thinking, "Oh good, today I can punish Bloggins! What horrible thing shall I do to him?"

The religious leaders did not like this idea better however. They hated the fact that the people now listened to Jesus and not to them, so they plotted to kill him.

They decided to arrest Jesus at night, when hardly anyone would be around to protest. That evening, Jesus and his disciples had a meal together. We call it the Last Supper, as it was the last meal Jesus ate before he died the next day.

Bloggins looked shocked. "But surely he was given breakfast!" he exclaimed.

Dr Maggins tried to explain that conditions for prisoners in first century Israel were not much like a B&B.

At the end of the meal, Jesus asked his disciples to eat some bread and drink some wine in memory of his body and blood, which he was about to sacrifice when he was killed. But of course they didn't understand what he was talking about.

Afterwards, they all went outside to a garden called the Garden of Gethsemane. Jesus was very upset, as he knew that it would not be long before he was killed by being nailed to a cross, a horrible punishment known as crucifixion. He began to talk to God, telling Him that he really didn't fancy being crucified and asking if he might not have to be. When you're scared, you'll know that it is comforting to have your friends round you, saying things like "Don't worry - it probably won't be so bad," and Jesus turned to his disciples, hoping they would say cheering things like this to him.

"It was very late," explained Dr Maggins, "and the disciples had drunk a lot of wine during the meal. So what do you think they were doing?"

Bloggins thought about his dad, who quite often came home from the pub or an office party having drunk too much.

"Throwing up?" he suggested.

"What an interesting idea," replied Dr Maggins, thinking that it certainly was interesting what you could learn about pupils' home lives from the things they said in class. "No, actually they weren't doing that. They had gone to sleep."

Bloggins was not surprised to hear this. His dad often did go to sleep when he had had a lot to drink and it could be difficult to wake him up.

Jesus was disappointed that his friends could not manage to stay awake even for one hour to support him. But soon everyone was awake, because a whole crowd of noisy men turned up. They had come to arrest Jesus.

The class looked shocked when they heard this, and hoped that Jesus would be able to escape. There was no time to hear what happened next, however, as the bell rang for assembly. As Bloggins lined up to go upstairs, he did not know who to be more worried about: Jesus or Bernie.

"I don't like to leave Bernie while he looks so uncomfortable," he complained. "Can Bliggins and I miss assembly and stay with him?"

"What a good idea," said Bliggins at once. "We could bring Finn the Fan over to stand near Bernie and try to cool him down. And then we could search the room for some coffee to cheer him up. I don't mind missing assembly."

"How very kind of you," said Dr Maggins. "But you don't need to worry. I will make sure that Bernie is feeling better by the time you get back."

The two boys looked disappointed, but had no option but to follow the class up to assembly. As they sang the hymn, "When I needed a neighbour", Bloggins couldn't help writing an extra verse in his head: "I was hot, I was sunburnt, were you there? Were you there?" and felt sad that he could not be there for Bernie.

When assembly was over, the children came hurriedly back to the classroom, anxious to see how Bernie was feeling. As they looked eagerly over to where Bernie sat at the front of the room, they gasped in surprise. Their beloved teacher Dr Maggins had indeed fulfilled her promise to make sure he was feeling better. Bernie was back to his old grey self.

"It's a miracle!" exclaimed Bloggins. "Just like the miracles that Jesus did!"

Everyone gathered round Bernie, searching for coffee and pencil sharpenings on the carpet to give him as a way of saying how pleased they were to see him well again.

No one ever knew what medicines or lotions Dr Maggins had used. If they had done, they would have suggested to the class next door that they use them on their bin, who seemed to have been out in the sun during assembly.

Chapter 10 - Rudy the Rubber gets Eaten

It was nearly the end of term and it was Bloggins' job that week to make sure everything in the classroom was tidy before he went home. That evening, he did so particularly carefully. He knew his mum was waiting to take him to the dentist, but he thought it was important to make sure first that the classroom was as tidy as it could be.

Some children had been drawing pictures when they had come in early from Games and there were pieces of crumpled paper and a few stray crayons lying around. Bloggins gave the paper to Rodders. Then he opened the desk drawer to give the crayons to Furry Bag. Furry Bag had only just gone back to sleep after a tiring afternoon, so he was not very pleased about being woken up and having his tummy opened again. But he was grateful for the crayons.

Peter Pan the Pen was lying on the desk. He was also feeling tired, having written "Good" on lots of pieces of work, but Dr Maggins had not yet put him to bed in Horace the Handbag. Bloggins knew that he absolutely mustn't open Horace, so he just laid Peter Pan the Pen carefully on top of him.

Next, Bloggins found that some of the children who had been given stars that day had left lots of coffee lying about on the side and the floor. He picked it all up and gave it to Bernie. Finally, he found some spare worksheets that were left over from the English lesson and he gave them to Drew the Drawer. Drew was pleased, as he had lost much of his paper to the children who came in early from Games.

By this time, Bloggins' mum was getting impatient and had come to look for him. She stormed into the room, tapping her watch.

"There you are, Bloggins!" she said angrily. "What on earth are you doing? We shall be late for the dentist. Come along right now!"

"But I haven't finished tidying the room," wailed Bloggins.

"It looks tidy enough to me," snapped his mum. "Come with me at once."

She took hold of Bloggins' hand. But Bloggins had seen another job that urgently needed doing. The whiteboard was covered with sums which the Maths teacher had written there when she was explaining long division. Bloggins picked up Rudy the Board Rubber and started to clean the board with his free hand. His mum had other ideas though. She pulled Bloggins away with a "Leave that", and Bloggins had no choice but to follow her. Poor Rudy was dropped and, to his dismay, he fell into Bernie the Bin.

"Let me go!" shouted Bloggins. "Bernie is eating Rudy!"

"Nonsense," barked his mum, and there was nothing Bloggins could do to save Rudy.

During Chummy Chat the next day, Bloggins raised his hand sadly.

"A terrible thing happened yesterday," he began, and his eyes filled with tears.

"Oh dear, I'm very sorry to hear that," said his kindly teacher Dr Maggins. "Whatever could have been?"

"I was trying to clean the board and Rudy fell into Bernie," blurted out Bloggins. "My mum wouldn't let me do anything to save him, and look! Rudy has disappeared! Bernie has eaten him!"

Everyone looked in horror at the place where Rudy usually sat. He had indeed gone.

"Rudy is dead!" shouted Bliggins loudly and some of the children began to cry.

"Does anyone have any other Chummy Chat?" asked Dr Maggins, hoping to distract the children's attention from this dreadful event.

As she had expected, Blaggins put up his hand.

"We're going to Scunthorpe this weekend," he announced proudly.

"How interesting," said Dr Maggins. "Do tell us what you are planning to do while you're there."

"My Mum has invited Bliggins and his parents to come and have some tea with us," replied Blaggins. "They will be in the area staying with friends."

Bliggins looked horrified. He forgot the upsetting news about Rudy and called to Blaggins across the room.

"Oh God, surely not! I'm bored to death with hearing about Scunthorpe. Surely I haven't actually got to go there!"

"You shouldn't use God's name as a swear word," shouted Bloggins. "That's one of the Ten Commandments!" An argument broke out between the three boys. Wanting to put a stop to this, and at the same time relieved that Rudy had been forgotten, at least for the moment, Dr Maggins told everyone to line up for assembly.

When they returned, some of the children were still talking sadly about the awful thing that had happened to Rudy. Dr Maggins decided to tell a story about someone else who had died in a dreadful way, even more dreadful than what had happened to Rudy.

The religious leaders who had arrested Jesus were determined that he should be killed. There was no proper reason to condemn him to death, so they got people to make up false evidence and bullied the Roman Governor, Pontius Pilate, into saying they could go ahead and crucify him.

Pontius Pilate wasn't interested in Jesus. He didn't care if Jesus claimed to be the Son of God because he belonged to a religion that had different gods. But he wanted to keep the peace, so he said he washed his hands of the matter.

"My mum makes me wash my hands of any matter I get on them, like mud or dog sick," interrupted Bloggins.

Dr Maggins gave him a Look and carried on.

Jesus was made to carry a wooden cross up a hill and when he got to the top, some soldiers nailed him to it.

"As he looked down from the cross," said Dr Maggins, "he saw his mother crying, as your mother would be if you were being crucified, and he couldn't do anything to comfort her so he asked his friend John to look after her. Soon after that, Jesus died."

The children all looked dismayed. This certainly did seem to be a lot worse than what had happened to Rudy.

Jesus' friends were allowed to take his body down from the cross and put it in a tomb. We are used to digging holes to bury people…

"Or dogs," put in Bloggins, remembering the grave his dad had dug for dear Waggins a few months ago.

...but in those times, people were usually buried in caves. A huge boulder was rolled over the entrance to Jesus' tomb to keep his body safe. Then the disciples had to go home because the Sabbath, a weekly religious festival, was just starting.

All this happened on the day we now call Good Friday.

Bliggins snorted. "Not very good for Jesus," he said. Dr Maggins explained that it was good for Christians because they believe Jesus died so that their sins could be forgiven. He is often called the Lamb of God because, before this, people would kill an animal such as a lamb if they wanted to say sorry to God.

"But that doesn't mean that I can go into town, rob a bank and mug an old lady and it will be ok because my sins are forgiven," explained Dr Maggins. "It only works if we are sorry about things we've done wrong and are trying not to do them again."

The Sabbath lasted all through Saturday until the sun set, so it was only on the Sunday that Jesus' friends were allowed to go back to the tomb and do things that there hadn't been time for on Friday. The friends who went were women, and they found an amazing thing had happened. The big stone had been rolled away and Jesus' body had disappeared. Not only that but during the next few days several of Jesus' friends saw him alive. Christians therefore believe that Jesus rose from the dead. This is called the Resurrection.

"Will Rudy rise from the dead?" piped up Bloggins.

Dr Maggins did not answer the question directly, but she suggested that, if someone you love dies, you might just find you get a sign that they are still with you if you look and listen carefully with your heart as well as with your eyes and ears.

Chapter 11 - The Term Ends

The last day of term finally arrived. Bloggins had mixed feelings about breaking up for the holidays. It would certainly be good not to have to do any work and to have more time to play. But he knew he was going to miss his beloved teacher Dr Maggins and all his friends in the classroom.

His mum had said that he could have Bliggins and Blaggins over for some playdates during the holidays and maybe even a sleepover. When he asked her about his other classroom friends, mentioning Winston the Wedge, Fergal the Fire Extinguisher and Furry Bag as examples, she looked confused and didn't seem to think that playdates and sleepovers with them would be possible.

On the final morning of term, the children were told to have a really good tidy of the classroom and to make sure any rubbish was thrown away. Bernie the Bin, Rodders the Recycling Box and Drew the Drawer always looked forward to this sort of morning as they knew all sorts of exciting things would be coming their way.

Each of the children took out the trays in which they kept their belongings. Everything needed to be taken out and sorted. Bloggins started to look through what was in his tray. There were a lot of old worksheets, some pieces of rough paper on which he had written the first drafts of poems he had been asked to compose, and also a great many sweet and biscuit wrappers.

The worksheets were still flat and looked like new. Bloggins gave these to Drew the Drawer. He turned his attention to the rough paper and started to read his poems with admiration. Really he was quite a good poet, he thought. Here was a brilliant example of his skill. He had been asked to describe a sunny day, using similes and metaphors. His first draft read:

"I really really like the sun,
It's round and shiny like a bum."

He knew that a simile was when you said something was like something else, so he had not been able to understand why Dr Maggins had not been pleased with this poem and had made him rewrite it.

Here was another amazing effort, which Bloggins had composed when asked to write a poem about a favourite place he liked to go, trying to mention his five senses. He had chosen to describe the toilet in his house, as this was a wonderful place to go if you wanted to be alone. He was pleased with the way he had described what he could see and hear while he was in there, and he felt that the words he had used to describe what he could smell and feel were particularly descriptive. It had been very upsetting when Dr Maggins had made him screw the poem up and write another one about the school garden.

Bloggins unscrewed the piece of paper and several others containing poems that had also apparently not been satisfactory. He thought of taking them home to show his mum, but decided instead to give them to Rodders, who he felt sure would appreciate being shown what a great poet he was.

He turned his attention to the sweet wrappers. Bloggins was fond of sweets and biscuits. The school discouraged pupils from bringing them in, suggesting instead that they should bring pieces of fruit to eat at breaktime. Bloggins thought this was a ridiculous idea, and he had managed to smuggle in a good supply of sweets and biscuits in his bag every day. It was one of the reasons that Bliggins and Blaggins were so keen to be friends with him.

Bloggins gathered the wrappers up in his hands and took them over to where Bernie the Bin sat waiting.

"There you go, Bernie," he said, as he deposited the wrappers in Bernie the Bin's tummy. "Enjoy!"

He went back to his tray to fetch another handful. As he gave these to Bernie, he noticed that the poor bin's tummy was getting alarmingly full. Not many of the children were good at keeping their trays tidy and they were all having a good clear out of the rubbish that had built up. Although Bernie the Bin loved being given rubbish, he was beginning to feel decidedly unwell.

Just then, Bliggins came over with several pieces of screwed up wrapping paper, which had contained some Christmas presents months before. Without looking what he was doing, he tossed them into Bernie.

"Oh dear, Bernie's being sick!" called out Bloggins, rushing over to help him.

"Calpol, Calpol!" shouted Blaggins.

"It's too late for that," declared Dr Maggins, looking at the mess on the floor round Bernie. "Luckily the cleaners have left some sick bags for Bernie. Fetch one quickly please, Bloggins."

Bloggins found the pile of black bin bags in the corner. He brought one over and opened it up. He and Bliggins then held Bernie's head while he vomited up all the pencil shavings, sweet wrappers, broken DT models, pieces of polystyrene and screwed up wrapping paper that he had stuffed himself with during the morning. When at last he was empty, Bernie felt better.

"There's more of Bernie's sick on the floor," said Blaggins, and kindly offered to clear it up. He usually steered well clear when someone had been sick, but he was fond of Bernie and wanted to help him.

Soon the sick bag was almost full. Bloggins put it near to Bernie in case he needed it again while everyone was at assembly.

All the trays were now tidy and the children put them back in their slots, feeling pleased that they had been able to give Drew, Rodders and Bernie so much to enjoy. It was a pity Bernie had been sick, but Bloggins knew that too much enjoyment could have that effect and he had learned from experience that it was important not to get over-excited at parties.

The final assembly of term was always a Serious Occasion. There was a buzz of chatter as the children entered the room. In order to calm them down, the Head announced that he would lead them in a mindful exercise. He told them to focus on their breathing.

"We shall do a nine-eleven," he declared. "Begin."

Some of the staff looked alarmed, but Bloggins knew that the Head always got muddled about the name of this exercise and that what he actually meant was a seven-eleven, when you had to count seven as you breathed in and eleven as you breathed out. Despite the end of term excitement, everyone focused on doing the exercise and gradually the atmosphere became calmer.

Now that the children were settled, the Head began to read a Carefully Chosen passage from the Bible. In it, Jesus was telling people that they ought not to worry about things like what they should eat or what they should wear, as God knows what we all need and will look after us. As an example, Jesus advised his listeners to consider the lilies that grew in the fields. They did not have to do any work or make clothes for themselves and yet they always looked beautiful. Even the King was not as splendidly clothed as a lily. Jesus went on to say that, if God looks after the birds and the plants, we can be confident that He will always look after us. So we should not be anxious and say things like, "What shall we eat?" or "What shall we wear?" We just need to have faith in God.

When he had finished the reading, the Head looked round encouragingly at the children. However, almost immediately, his smile faded and a frown took its place.

"Oh dear," he remarked. "I can see that many of you think that because it is the end of term, you can let standards slip. You are looking very scruffy. Shirts are untucked and a lot of the boys are not wearing ties. If you are not wearing a tie, please stay behind afterwards and explain yourselves."

Bloggins frowned slightly. Somehow the Head's words did not seem to go with the Bible reading, though he could not quite work out why. However, he soon forgot about this as everyone stood up to sing the hymn.

Because of the Seriousness of the Occasion, it was not one of the songs that Gordon the Guitar enjoyed, but a hymn called "Jerusalem", which the Music teacher accompanied on Oswald the Organ. It is a stirring hymn and everyone sang loudly. As it finished, some of the pupils who were leaving were in tears.

When the children got back to the classroom, Bloggins was relieved to see that Bernie had not been sick again. He did feel worried, though, that everyone was about to go home for the holidays and so many of his classroom friends would be left all alone.

How would Drew the Drawer and Rodders the Recycling Box feel if no one was giving them any paper?

Would Bernie the Bin starve without any rubbish or coffee?

Might Furry Bag feel lonely, stuck in the drawer all day?

Luckily, his thoughtful teacher Dr Maggins reassured the children that she would be coming into school regularly during the holidays and would make sure that no one there was unhappy. Gordon the Guitar would be spending the holidays at home with her anyway and would be really delighted with the boxes of chocolates that some of the children had brought to school for him that morning.

The children who had not brought any chocolate felt rather guilty and wondered whether they could get their mums to go away and buy some before Gordon had to leave.

There was just a little while left now until the final bell went and the children begged to be allowed to play a few rounds of "Heads down, thumbs up". For some reason that Dr Maggins could never fathom, they all loved this game, which consisted of closing your eyes and trying to guess who had touched your thumb.

Bloggins was very excited when he guessed correctly that Bliggins had touched his thumb, as this meant he could now take a turn at being one of the people who crept round the room and quietly touched a thumb.

Unfortunately, before there was time for his round to start, the bell rang. As he gathered up his things and staggered out of the room, somehow managing to keep hold of his bag, an enormous roll of artwork and a working model of a carousel, he thought what a wonderful term it had been. He had learnt so much about so many things. His favourite lessons had been about the Bible stories.

With some difficulty, Bloggins waved through the window at Bernie, Rodders, Frank, Drew, Winston and Finn. He called out,

"I'll be thinking of you all through the holidays!"

What a wonderful thing it was to know from his time in their classroom that he too would be remembered all through the holidays, and indeed forever.

Let's end the stories with pictures of some of the characters waving goodbye. Over to you…

Printed in Great Britain
by Amazon

45446271R00056